Cosmonaut and Taikonaut Autographs

An Identification Guidebook 1961-2018

JOHN R. MITCHELL

Dedication and Introduction

This book is dedicated to the many brave men and women who willingly risked their lives to explore the unknown beyond our world by strapping themselves on top of a rocket loaded with as much as 300,000 gallons of fuel and being launched into the realms of space.

Acknowledgements

I especially want to thank the late Lester Winick, who inspired me to collect Soviet space covers a long time ago (in a galaxy far away), and to the late Stephen Datz, who published an excellent identification book on cosmonaut autographs in 1994. Also, a very special thanks goes out to Robert McLeod for assisting with autograph scans from his website. Without Bob, this book would not be possible.

PART I

HOW THIS BOOK CAME TO BE

Recently I began sorting and identifying my collection of space covers and assorted autographs, and I came upon a number of autographed covers I had acquired in the early to mid '70's at various stamp shows I had attended and through mail auctions. Some covers had been marked with signing information, but a number of them were not. I had acquired many of these covers from dealers who had them, did not know who signed them, and threw them into their bargain bins as they were not in demand.

With the help of many searches on the Internet, I eventually determined the identity of the signers. I realized, however, that there were no really good current reference books in print identifying cosmonaut autographs. I did find a great book by Stephen Datz entitled "Cosmonaut Autographs" and printed by Sanabria, Loveland, Colorado in 1994, but I could not find anything in publication more current than this. Furthermore, that book has been out of print, Sanabria was out of business and Mr. Datz had passed on in 2015. Those of us who do not have a working knowledge of the Russian or Chinese languages have a tough time identifying what we have accumulated. And that's how this book came about; I needed a reference, and figured other collectors do also. I hope this guidebook is an effective and useful tool for you, the collector.

In this book, I am providing reproductions of the various space travelers' autographs. I have included a few signatures of US astronaut who flew with the cosmonauts, either in Soyuz or Space Shuttle vehicles which the collector may run across and find difficult to identify, but to include all of them is beyond the scope of this book.

Autograph authenticity is a prime concern to me and it should be with all collectors everywhere. I also must present a disclaimer here; I do not claim to be an expert on authenticating autographs. There are experts within the autograph collector field who specialize in this. I have a small collection compared to many collectors I have met.

COLLECTING COSMONAUT AND TAIKONAUT AUTOGRAPHS

Collecting anything usually begins when a person notices something that they take a liking to. It may be books, coins, antiques, stamps, record albums, US or world paper money, pottery, art, or autographs. Anything. Once we begin a collection, we accumulate what we like; items of interest to us. And that should be the way of this hobby, too. Do you like autographs on space-related envelopes (known as covers) or on photographs? Do you prefer space topical books? What about letters and other documents? Collect what you like, and enjoy your hobby.

Probably the most common cosmonaut signed items are photographs and covers. A *cover* is an envelope with a stamp affixed and canceled, and usually with a space-related illustration (a cachet) printed or stamped on it, such as a space mission, a space traveler, an anniversary or other event. The cover on the front of this book was canceled in the city of Riga on 1/1/1963 and signed by 17 of the first 22 Soviet cosmonauts. Can you identify them?

There are several types of covers available to collectors; an *event* cover, which notes a launch, a link-up or docking or a landing. *First day covers* (FDC) are produced on the first day of issue of a stamp, and usually say first day on the cover. There are many dealers and other sellers who incorrectly refer to **all** space covers as FDC, rather than event covers.

Older covers from the former Soviet Union were generally produced in the "European" size envelope. The USSR issued many stamped envelopes with space themes, and these were frequently used. Newer covers seem to be going to the longer and narrower envelope. And with the invention of computers and personal printers, there are some very sophisticated covers being produced today.

Signed photos are the second most frequently encountered collectable. In the US, 8 x 10 photos are the most common, but in other parts of the world, smaller photos are more frequent; 4x6, 5x7 or postcard sized photographs.

Many collectors I know collect all items (generally, anything they can get their hands on!).

Photographs are available as portraits, crews, and snapshots of the crews in action both on the ground and in space. Again, collect what suites you.

Many of the current space travelers can be reached through the mail or in person at stamp shows, space symposiums, speaking appearances, etc. and will sign items for the fan or collectors. But **always** be courteous and polite, as these people are not obliged in any way to give or send an autograph. Also, limit what you send to two or three items, and include a stamped addressed envelope. I have heard many stories about collectors being rude and demanding signatures, or dealers sending in twenty or more items to sign, and these individuals ruin the hobby for everyone else.

WHAT IS MY ITEM WORTH?

This may be the most frequently asked question about autographs. The answer varies greatly. An autograph is worth only what someone else is willing to pay for it. Much of course depends upon the scarcity of the item. Yuri Gagarin was the first man in space in 1961, and died in a plane crash in 1968. He reportedly signed a great deal of items, but there is also a huge demand for his autograph. I have seen asking prices range from $250 to over $2000, depending on what was offered. International Space Station visitors' autographs can range from just a few dollars to several hundred, again depending upon what is signed and how scarce these are. It all depends upon supply and demand. Combinations of the different space travelers on photographs or covers can add value (i.e. Gagarin and Gherman Titov or Gagarin and Tereshkova together would be much more valuable to a collector than as separate items).

You should also consider the condition of the item; is the photograph nice and crisp, or is it faded, bent or torn corners, have pinholes in it or have folds or creases? Is the autograph clear, or is it light or smudged?

The early cosmonauts did not sign any souvenirs before they flew in space for the first time, either from government policy, or from tradition carried over from WW I military pilots. Also, the names of the space travelers were not announced in advance of their flights. That has changed today.

SECRETARIAL SIGNATURES, FAKES AND AUTOPENS

Most cosmonaut autographs today are moderately priced, and there are very few fakes of the inexpensive autographs on the market. I do not know of any of the cosmonauts using a secretary to sign items, unlike the western world, especially in entertainment and sports, where secretarials and preprints abound. That being said, you need to be careful with the more expensive and scarce items. I have seen some very questionable Gagarin autographs being offered on ebay in recent years. Also, a number of the newer cosmonauts' autographs can be copied (forged) very easily. So, whether you are purchasing from a dealer or an individual, be certain the seller has an impeccable reputation, and be certain of the provenance of the autograph you are buying.

I know there are many fake Gagarin autographs on the market. Gagarin signed many items during his lifetime (He died in a plane crash in 1968) but there is such a demand for his autograph that asking prices can be in three and four figures. Tereshkova, on the other hand, has made some appearance, but has been very reluctant to sign through the mail. And with the Soyuz 11 crew perishing upon re-entry from space in 1971, Viktor Patsayev and Georgy Dobrovolsky autographs are very rare, as the Soviet government kept crew selection secret, only announcing after their launch who was on board. As this was their first flight, probably the only autographs available would be from personal correspondence. Signatures on collector type items are unknown. The third crewman, Vladislav Volkov, had flown one mission before, Soyuz 7 in 1969, so his autograph is available, but in very limited quantities and commands a premium.

I have read that cosmonauts who worked with this crew in 1971 stated they did not know of any covers these men signed prior to launch of Soyuz 11.

This cover was submitted recently as an example of the Soyuz 11* crew autographs along with other cosmonauts. The listing, in order:

Alexei Yeliseyev: Soyuz 5, 8 and 10

(*) Vladislav Volkov: Soyuz 7 and 11

Georgi Beregovoy: Soyuz 3 (deceased)

(*) Victor Patsayev: Soyuz 11

(*) Georgi Dobrovolsky: Soyuz 11

Anatoly Filipchenko: Soyuz 7 and 16

Pavel Popovich: Vostok 4 and Soyuz 14 (deceased)

The decision of a number of space cover collectors who have examined this cover is that the signatures look "heavy-handed and miss the dynamics of their natural signatures." The consensus is that they are fakes. An article I've read claims that Alexei Leonov, who was commander of the original crew selected for Soyuz 11, and then bumped, stated he did not know of any covers signed by the two men prior to their mission. The expert collectors consider these signatures to be questionable; especially those of the Soyuz 11 mission. Are they all faked? I do not know, but suspect that they are.

This uncanceled cover is reportedly signed by A. Leonov, P. Kolodin, and V. Kubasov, the original team selected for Soyuz 11, but who were replaced due to exposure to tuberculosis, and also signed by the perished replacement team of G. Dobrovolsky, V. Volkov, and V. Patsayev. Again, I do not know if these autographs are genuine or fakes. This was offered by Auctionshaus Felzmann on the Stamp Auction Network, lot 3760 in March of 2018 but did not sell (it may have been withdrawn or had a minimum starting bid of $22,000 that was too high). A Russian dealer under the name "Maksuta" sold large quantities of fake Soyuz 11 covers, photos and postcards years ago.

Fortunately for collectors, the Soviet Union and modern day Russia have not provided cosmonauts with an autopen devise to mechanically reproduce autographs. Cosmonauts who train in the United States have been given access of the autopen by NASA during their training, and there are a few autopen signatures that have reached the hands of fans and collectors. I have not seen any examples of secretarial autographs.

So the final word is; let the buyer beware! An astute autograph collector is one who, when he finds an autograph, must *question* the item, assume it is *not genuine*, *research* it, and then *prove* it to be authentic. And if you are offered a cover similar to the first one above, **do not buy it! Buyer Beware!**

PART II

Autographs of Cosmonauts from Russia, Intercosmos Astronauts, Eastern Europe (ESA), Japanese and select US Astronauts with signatures difficult to identify

Please remember that each person's autograph differs each time they sign something. They often differ in size and shape, and much depends upon where they are at time of signing. The examples shown here are samples only to help you identify the person's signature with relative ease. If you find two autographs that are identical, that means they were mechanically reproduced (copied). I have not included unflown backup cosmonauts. These signatures are presented mainly as examples and not necessarily for authentication purposes, but to the best of my knowledge, they are authentic I am also including some select US and ESA astronauts with autographs difficult to identify. I am not listing **Viktor Patsayev** and **Georgy Dobrovolsky** here, as I have not seen examples of their autographs certified as genuine. I am including the cosmonauts' names in Russian and other native languages where available to assist in identification.

Afansayev, Viktor (Soyuz TM-11, TM-18, TM-29, TM-33/TM-32) Виктор Афанасьев

Aimbetov, Aidyn (Kazakh) (Soyuz TMA-18M / TMA-16M) Айдын Айымбетов

Akiyama, Toyohiro (Japan) (Soyuz TM-11/ TM-10) signatures in Japanese and Russian) 秋山 豊寛

Aksyonov, Vladimir (Soyuz 22, T-2) Влади́мир Аксёнов

Alexandrov, Alexandr Panayotov (Bulgaria) (Soyuz TM-5/ TM-4) Александър
Александров

Alexandrov, Alexandr Pavlovich (Russia) (Soyuz T-9, TM-3) Александр Павлович
Александров

Andre-Deshays, Claudie (Haigneré) (France) (Soyuz TM-24/TM-23,TM-33/ TM-32)

From Daughter of Iran to Space Pioneer

Anousheh Ansari

Ansari, Anousheh (Iranian-American space tourist) (Soyuz TMA-8/ TMA-9)

Artsebarsky, Anatoly (Soyuz TM-12) Анатолій Арцебарський

Artemyev, Oleg (Soyuz MS-08, TMA-12M) Олег Артемьев

Artyukin, Yuri (Soyuz 14) ++ 8/4/1998 Юрий Артю́хин

Atkov, Oleg (Soyuz T-11/T-10) Оле́г Атько́в

Aubakarov, Toktar (Ukraine) (Soyuz TM-13/TM-12) Тоқтар Әубәкіров

Avdeyev, Sergei (Soyuz TM-29/TM-28, TM-22, TM-15) Сергей Авдеев

Balandin, Alexander (Soyuz TM-9) Александр Баландин

Baturin, Yuri (Soyuz TM-28, TM-31, TM-27, TM-32) Юрий Батурин

Bella, Ivan (Czechoslovakia) (Soyuz TM-29/TM-28)

Belyayev, Pavel (Voskhod 2) ++ (died 1/10/1970 after surgery Павел Беляев

Beregovoy, Georgi (Ukraine) (Soyuz 3) ++ 6/30/1995 Гео́ргий Берегово́й

Berezovoy, Anatoly (Soyuz T-5/T-7) ++ 9/20/2014 Анато́лий Березово́й

Borisenko, Andrei (Soyuz MS-02, MS-14, TMA-21) *Андрей Борисенко*

Budarin, Nikolai (STS-71, STS-113, Soyuz TMA-1, TM-27, TM-21) Николай Бударин

Bykovsky, Valery (Vostok 5, Salyut 6, Soyuz 31, 22, 29) Валéрий Быкóвский

Chang-Diaz, Franklin (USA) (STS-75, 61-C, 34, 111, 91, 60, 46) Not a cosmonaut, but an unusual autograph.

Chretien, Jean-Loup (France) (Soyuz T-6, TM-7/ TM-6, STS-86)

Creamer, Tim (USA) (Soyuz TMA-17)

Союз ТМА-15М

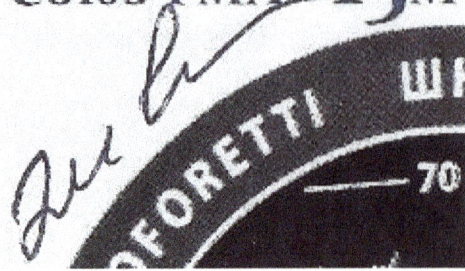

Cristoforetti, Samantha (Italy) (Soyuz TMA-15M)

Demin, Lev (Sometimes spelled Dyomin) (Soyuz 15) ++ 12/18/1998 Лев Дёмин

Dezhurov, Vladimir (Soyuz TM-21, STS-71, STS-105, STS-108) Влади́мир Дежу́ров

Duque, Pedro (Spain) (STS-95, Soyuz TMA-3/TMA-2)

Dzhanibekov, Vladimir (Soyuz 27/26, 39, T-6, T-12, T-13) Владимир Джанибеков

Faris, Mohammed (Syria) (Soyuz TM-3/TM-2) فــارس أحمد محمد

Farkas, Bertalan (Hungary) (Soyuz 35)

Feoktistov, Konstantin (Voskhod 1) ++ 11/21/2009 Константин Феоктистов

Feustel, Andrew (USA) (Soyuz MS-08)

Filipchenko, Anatoly (Soyuz 7, 16) Анато́лий Фили́пченко

Fincke, Michael (Soyuz TMA-4, TMA-13)

Flade, Klaus-Dietrich (Germany) (Soyuz TM-14/TM-13)

Furukawa, Satoshi (Japan) (Soyuz TMA-02M)

Gagarin, Yuri (Vostok 1) ++ 3/27/1968 (Caution: dangerous fakes exist) Юрий Гага́рин

ESA ASCAN, 2009

Gerst, Alexander (Germany) (Soyuz TMA-13M, MS-09)

Gidzenko, Yuri (Soyuz TM-22, TM-31/STS-102, Soyuz TM-34/TM-33) Юрий Гидзенко

Glazkov, Yuri (Soyuz 24) ++ 12/9/2008 Юрий Глазко́в

Gorbatko, Viktor (Soyuz 7, 24, 37/36) ++ 5/15/2017 Виктор Горбатко

Grechko, Georgy (Soyuz 17, 26/27, T-14/T-13) ++ 4/8/2017 Георгий Гречко

Gubarev, Alexei (Soyuz 17, 28) ++ 2/21/2015 Алексей Губарев

Gürragchaa, Jügderdemidiin (Mongolia) (Soyuz 39) Жугдэрдэмидийн Гуррагча

Haigneré, Jean-Pierre (France) (Soyuz TM-17/TM-16, TM-29)

Hermaszewski, Mlroslaw (Poland) (Soyuz 30)

Ivanchenkov, Alexander (early and later) (Soyuz 29/31, T-6) Алекса́ндр Иванче́нков

Ivanishin, Anatoli (Soyuz TMA-22, MS-01) Анатолий Иванишин

(signature) 21.06.84

Ivanov, Georgi {Bulgaria) (Soyuz 33) Георги Какалов

(signature: Sigmund Jähn) _(signature: S. Jähn)_

Jähn, Sigmund (Germany) (Soyuz 31/29)

(signature: Leonid K. Kadenyuk "STS-87 PS") _(signature) STS-87_

Kadenyuk, Leonid (Ukraine) (STS-87) ++ 1/31/2018 Леонід Каденюк

(signature) „Союз ТМ-14" космонавт

Kaleri, Aleksandr (Soyuz TM-14, TM-24, TM-30, TMA-3, TMA-01M) Александр Калери

Kelly, James (USA) (STS-104, STS-112)

Kelly, Scott (USA) (STS-103, STS-118, Soyuz TMA-01M, TMA-16M, TMA-18M)

Khrunov, Yevgeny (Soyuz 5/4) ++ 5/19/2000 Евгéний Хрунóв

Kizim, Leonid (Soyuz T-3, T-10/T-11, T-15) ++ 6/14/2010 Леонид Кизим

Klimuk, Pyotr (Belarus) (Soyuz 13, 18, 30) Пётр Клімук

Komarov, Vladimir (scarce; authentication recommended) (Soyuz 1, Voskhod 1) ++ 4/24/1967
Влади́мир Комаро́в

Kondakova, Yelena (Soyuz TM-20, STS-84) Елена Кондако́ва

Kondratyev, Dmitri (Soyuz TMA-20) Дмитрий Кондратьев

Кононенко
(class of (1996)

Kononenko, Oleg (Soyuz TMA-12, TMA-03M, TMA-17M) Олег Кононенко

М. Корн

Korniyenko, Mikhail (Soyuz TMA-18, TMA-16M/TMA-18M) Михаил Корниенко

32815

В. Корзун

8.05.03

Korzun, Valery (Soyuz TM-24, STS-111, STS-113) Валерий Корзун

Котов
Олег
Валериевич

Kotov, Oleg (Ukraine) (Soyuz TMA-10, TMA-17, TMA-10M) Олег Котов

Kovalyonok, Vladimir (Soyuz 25, 29/31, T-4) Владимир Ковалёнок

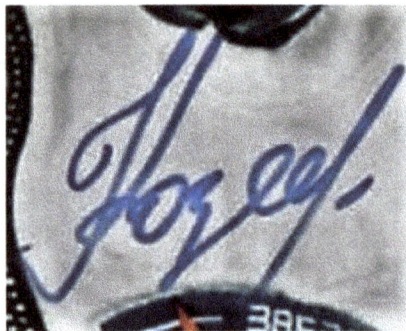

Kozeyev, Konstantin (Belarus) (Soyuz TM-33/TM-32) Константин Козеев

Flown Soyuz TM₁₂
— MIR
KRIKALEV

Krikalev, Sergei (Soyuz TM-7, TM-12/TM-13, STS-60, STS-88, TM-31/STS-102, TMA-6) Сергей Крикалёв

Kubasov, Valery (Soyuz 6, 19[ASTP], 36) ++ 2/19/2014 Валéрий Кубáсов

Kuipers, Andre (Netherlands) (Soyuz TMA-4/TMA-3, TMA-03M)

Laliberte, Guy (Canada) (Soyuz TMA-16/14) Note: many variations exist

Laveykin, Alexander (Soyuz TM-2) Александр Лавейкин

Lazarev, Vasily (Soyuz 12, 18a) ++ 12/31/1990 Васи́лий Ла́зарев

[signature]

Cosmonaut
" Soyuz - TM-25

Lazutkin, Aleksandr (Soyuz TM-25) Александр Лазуткин

[signature]

Lebedev, Valentin (Soyuz 13, T-5/T-7) Валентин Лебедев

[signature]

Leonov, Alexei (Voskhod 2, Soyuz 19[ASTP]) Алексе́й Лео́нов

[signature]

Levchenko, Anatoly (Anatoly died some eight months after his only flight. His autograph is the third scarcest of the cosmonauts. Watch for forgeries.) (Soyuz TM-4/TM-3) ++ 8/6/1988 Анатолий Левченко

Lindgren, Kjell (USA) (Soyuz TMA-17M)

Lonchakov, Yury (STS-100, Soyuz TMA-1/TM-34, TMA-13) Юрий Лончаков

Lyakhov, Vladimir (Soyuz 32, T-9, TM-6/TM-5) ++ 4/19/2018 Влади́мир Ля́хов

Makarov, Oleg (Soyuz 7, 12, 27/26, T-3) ++ 5/28/2003 Оле́г Мака́ров

Ю. малекко

мир - 16

Malenchenko, Yuri (Soyuz TM-19, STS-106, Soyuz TMA-2, TMA-11, TMA-05M, TMA-19M)
Юрий Маленченко

Yuri Malyshev

5.04.85.

Malyshev, Yuri (Soyuz T-2, T-11/T-10) ++ 11/8/1999 Ю́рий Ма́лышев

Manakov, Gennedi (Soyuz TM-10, TM-16) Геннадий Манаков

Manarov, Musa (Azerbaijan) (Soyuz TM-4/TM-6), Soyuz TM-11) Муса Манаров

Misurkin, Alexander (Soyuz TMA-08M, MS-06) Александр Мисуркин

Mohmand, Abdul Ahad (Afghanistan}(Soyuz TM-6/TM-5) مومند عبدالاحـد

Morukov, Boris (STS-106) ++ 1/1/2015 Борис Моруков

Musabayev, Talgat (Kazakhstan) (Soyuz TM-19, TM-27, TM-32/TM-31) Талғат Мұсабаев

Nikolayev, Andrian (Vostok 3, Soyuz 9) ++ 7/3/2004 Андриян Николаев

Noguchi, Soichi (Japan) (STS-114, Soyuz TMA-17)

Novitski, Oleg (Soyuz TMA-06M, MS-03) Олег Новицкий

Onishi, Takuya (Japan) (Soyuz MS-01, TMA-20M) 大西 卓哉

Onufrienko, Yury (Ukraine) (Soyuz TM-23, STS-108, STS-111) Юрий Онуфриенко

Ovchinin
Aleksei Nikolaevych

Ovchinin, Aleksey (Soyuz TMA-20M) Алексей Овчинин

Gennady Padalka
Soyuz -TM-28
"MIR-26"

Padalka, Gennady (Soyuz TM-28, TMA-4, TMA-14, TMA-04M, TMA-16M) Геннадий
Падалка

Perrin, Phillipe (France) (STS-111)

Pesquet, Thomas (France) (Soyuz MS-03)

Poleshchuk, Alexander (Soyuz TM-16) Александр Полещук

Polyakov, Valeri (Soyuz TM-6/ TM-7, TM-18/TM-20) Валерий Поляко

To Robert McLeod, Best Wishes,

Pontes, Marcos (Brazil) (Soyuz TMA-8/TMA-7)

Popov, Leonid (Soyuz 35/37, 40, T-7/T-5) Леонйд Попóв

Popovich, Pavel (Ukraine) (Vostok 4, Soyuz 14) ++ 9/29/2009 Пáвел Попóвич

Prunariu, Dumitru (Romania) (Soyuz 40)

Remek, Vladimir (Czechoslovakia) (Soyuz 28)

Revin, Sergei (Soyuz TMA-04M) Сергей Ревин

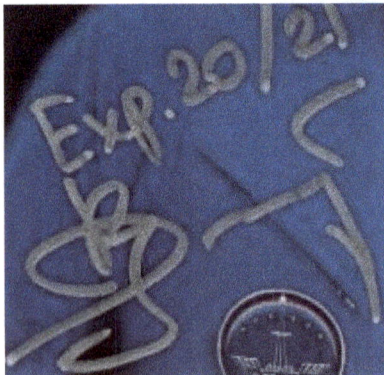

Romanenko, Roman (Soyuz TMA-15, TMA-07M) Wide variations exist. Роман Романенко

Romanenko, Yuri (Soyuz 26/27, 38, TM-2/TM-3) Ю́рий Романе́нко

Rozhdestvensky, Valery (Soyuz 23) ++ 8/31/2011 Валерий Рождественский

Rukavishnikov, Nikolai (Soyuz 10, 16, 33) ++ 10/18/2002 Никола́й Рукави́шников

Ryazanski, Sergey (Soyuz TMA-10M, MS-05) Сергéй Рязанский

Ryumin, Valery (Soyuz 25, 32, 35/37, 34, STS-91) Валерий Рюмин

Ryzhikov, Sergey (Soyuz MS-02) Сергей Рыжиков

Samokutyayev, Aleksandr (Soyuz TMA-21, TMA-14M) Александр Самокутяев

Sarafanov, Gennadi (Soyuz 15) ++ 9/29/2005 Геннадий Сарафанов

Savinykh, Viktor (Soyuz T-4, T-13, TM-5/TM-4) Виктор Савиных

Savitskaya, Svetlana ((Soyuz T-7/T-5, T-12) Светлáна Савѝцкая

Serebrov, Alexander (Soyuz T-7/T-5, T-8, TM-8, TM-17) ++ 11/12/2013 Алекса́ндр Серебро́в

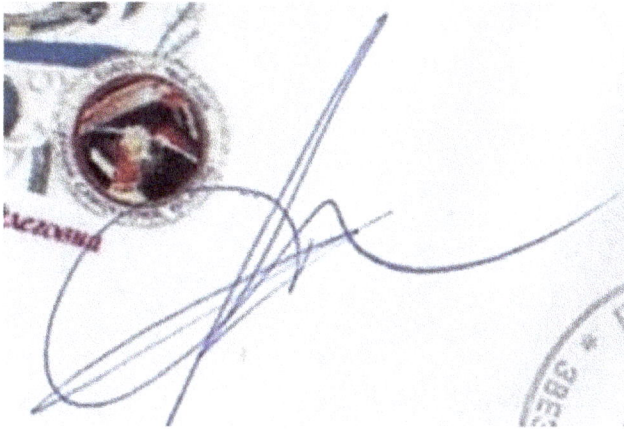

Serova, Yelena (Soyuz TMA-14M) Елена Серова

Sevastyanov, Vitaly (Soyuz 9, Soyuz 18) ++ 4/5/2010 Вита́лий Севастья́нов

Shargin, Yuri (Soyuz TMA-5, TMA-4) Юрий Шаргин

Sharipov, Salizhan (STS-89, Soyuz TMA-5) Салижан Шарипов

Sharma, Rakesh (India) (Soyuz T-11/T-10)

Sharman, Helen (Great Britain) (Soyuz TM-12/ TM-11)

Shatalov, Vladimir (Soyuz 4, 8, 10) Владимир Шаталов

Shkaplerov, Anton (Soyuz TMA-22, TMA-15M, MS-07) Антон Шкаплеров

Shonin, Georgi (Ukraine) (Soyuz 6) ++ 4/7/1997 Гео́ргій Шо́нін

Shukor, Sheikh Muszaphar (Malaysia) (Soyuz TMA-11/TMA-10)

Shuttleworth, Mark (USA) (Soyuz TM-34/TM-33)

Simonyi, Charles (Hungarian-American) (Soyuz TMA-10/9, TMA-14/13)

Скрипочка Олег Иванович
Skripochka Oleg Ivanovich

бортинженер / Flight Engineer

Skripochka, Oleg (Soyuz TMA-01M, TMA-20M) Оле́г Скри́почка

Skvortsov, Aleksandr (Soyuz TMA-18, MS-13, TMA-12M) Александр Скворцов

Solovyov, Anatoly (Soyuz TM-5/TM-4, TM-9, TM-15, STS-71/ TM-21, TM-26) Анатолий Соловьёв

Solovyov, Vladimir (Soyuz T-10/T-11, T-15) Влади́мир Соловьёв

Strekalov, Gennadi (Soyuz T-3, T-8, T-10-1, T-11/TM-10, TM-21/STS-71) ++ 12/25/2004
Генна́дий Стрека́лов

Surayev, Maksim (Soyuz TMA-16, TMA-13M) Макси́м Сура́ев

Tamayo-Méndez, Arnaldo (Cuba) (Soyuz 38

Tarelkin, Evgeny (Soyuz TMA-06M) Евгений Тарелкин

Tereshkova, Valentina (Vostok 6) Валенти́на Терешко́ва

Tingle, Scott (USA) (Soyuz MS-07)

Tito, Dennis (USA) (Soyuz TM-32/TM-31)

Titov, Gherman (Vostok 2) ++ 9/20/2000 Герман Титов

Titov, Vladimir (Russian and English versions) (Soyuz T-8, T-10-1, TM-4/TM-6, STS-63, STS-86) Владимир Титов

Tognini, Michel (France) (STS-93, Soyuz TM-14/TM-15)

Tokarev, Valeri (STS-96, Soyuz TMA-7) Валерий Токарев

Treshchyov, Sergei (STS-111/STS-113) Сергей Трещёв

Tsibliyev, Vasily (Soyuz TM-17, TM-25) Василий Циблие

Tuan, Pham (Vietnam) (Soyuz 36/37)

Tyurin, Mikhail (STS-105/STS-108, Soyuz TMA-9, TMA-11M) Михаил Тюрин

Usachev, Yuri (Soyuz TM-18, TM-23, STS-101, STS-102/STS-105) Юрий Усачёв

Vasyutin, Vladimir (Soyuz T-14) ++July 19, 2002 Владимир Васютин

Viehböck, Franz (Austria) (Soyuz TM-13/TM-12)

Viktorenko, Alexander (Soyuz TM-3/TM-2, TM-8, TM-14, TM-20) Александр Викторенко

Vinogradov, Pavel (Soyuz TM-26, TMA-8, TMA-08M) Павел Виноградов

Vittori, Roberto (Italy) (STS-134, Soyuz TMA-6/TMA-5, TM-34/TM-33)

Volk, Igor (Soyuz T-12) ++ 1/3/2017 Игорь Волк

Volkov, Alexander (Soyuz T-14, TM-7, TM-13) Алекса́ндр Во́лков

Volkov, Sergey Note the similarities between Sergey's and Alexander's autograph (above). Sergey is Alexander's son.
(Soyuz TMA-12, TMA-02M, TMA-18M) Сергей Волков

Volkov, Vladislav (Caution: dangerous forgeries exist) (Soyuz 7, 11) ++ 6/29/1971 Владисла́в
Во́лков

Volynov, Boris (Soyuz 5, 21) Бори́с Воль́нов

Williams, Sunita (USA) (STS-116/STS-117, Soyuz TMA-05M)

Wiseman, Gregory (USA) (Soyuz TMA-13M)

Yegorov, Boris (Voskhod 1) ++ 9/12/1994 Борис Егоров

Yeliseyev, Alexei (Soyuz 5/4, 8, 10) Алексей Елисеев

Yi, So-yeon (South Korea) (Soyuz TMA-12/TMA-11) 이 소 연

Yui, Kimiya (Japan) Two versions of his autograph (Soyuz TMA-17M) 油井 亀美也

Yurchikhin, Fyodor (STS-112, TMA-10, TMA-19, TMA-09M, Soyuz MS-04 Фёдор Юрчихин

Zalyotin, Sergei (**S**oyuz TM-30, TMA-1/TM-34) Сергéй Залётин

Zholobov, Vitaly (Soyuz 21) Виталий Жолобов

Zudov, Vyacheslav (Soyuz 23) Вячеслáв Зýдов

++ indicates person is deceased, with day of death given

When a mission is shown as split, such as (Soyuz TM-32/TM-31), this indicates the space traveler was launched onboard one space vehicle and returned to Earth via another.

PART III

COSMONAUT MISSIONS AND CREWS 1961-1985

VOSTOK PROGRAM

VOSTOK 1 **Gagarin**, Yuri	Ascent & descent date: April 12, 1961 (Made 1 revolution around the Earth)
VOSTOK 2 **Titov**, Gherman	Ascent date: August 6, 1961 Descent date: August 7, 1961
VOSTOK 3 **Nikolayev**, Andriyan	Ascent date: August 11, 1962 Descent date: August 15, 1962
VOSTOK 4 **Popov**, Pavel	Ascent date: August 12, 1962 Descent date: August 15, 1962 (came within 6.5 km (4.0 mi) of Vostok 3)
VOSTOK 5 **Bykovsky**, Valery	Ascent Date: 14 June 1963 Descent date: 19 June 1963
VOSTOK 6 **TERESHKOVA**, Valentina	Ascent Date: 16 June 1963 Descent date: 19 June 1963 (Rendezvous with Vostok 5)

VOSKHOD PROGRAM

VOSKHOD 1 Crew **Komorov**, Vladimir **Feoktistov**, Konstantin **Yegorov**, Boris	Ascent Date: 12 October 1964 Descent date: 13 October 1964 (First 3-man crew in space)
VOSKHOD 2 Crew **Belyayev**, Pavel **Leonov**, Alexey	Ascent Date: March 18, 1965 Descent date: March 19, 1965 (1st space walk)

SOYUZ PROGRAM

SOYUZ 1   Ascent date: April 23, 1967
Komarov, Vladimir   Descent date: April 24, 1967
Komarov died upon re-entry of the spacecraft.

SOYUZ 2   Ascent date: August 25, 1968
Unmanned - was to be target spaceship for Soyuz 3 rendezvous

SOYUZ 3   Ascent date: October 25, 1968
Beregovoy, Georgi   Descent date: October 30, 1968

SOYUZ 4   Ascent date: January 14, 1969
Ascending crew   Docked with Soyuz 5
Shatalov, Vladimir
Descending crew   Descent date: January 17, 1969
Khrunov, Yevgeny (Soyuz 5)
Shatalov, Vladimir (Soyuz 4)
Yeliseyev, Alexei (Soyuz 5)

SOYUZ 5   Ascent date: January 15, 1969
Ascending crew
Khrunov, Yevgeny
Yeliseyev, Alexei
Volynov, Boris
Descending crew   Descent date: January 16, 1969
Volynov, Boris

SOYUZ 6   Ascent date: October 11, 1969
Crew   Descent date: October 16, 1969
Kubasov, Valeri
Shonin, Georgy
Scheduled docking was not accomplished

SOYUZ 7   Ascent date: October 12, 1969
Crew   Descent date: October 17, 1969
Filipchenko, Anatoly
Gorbatko, Viktor
Volkov, Vladislav
Scheduled docking was not accomplished

SOYUZ 8
Crew
Shatalov, Vladimir
Yeliseyev, Alexei

Ascent date: October 13, 1969
Descent date: October 18, 1969

SOYUZ 9
Crew
Nikolayev, Andriyan
Sevastyanov, Vitaly

Ascent date: June 1, 1970
Descent date: June 19, 1970

SALYUT 1 SPACE STATION
Unmanned launch: April 19, 1971   Reentry: October 11, 1971

SOYUZ 10 TO SALYUT 1
Crew
Shatalov, Vladimir
Yeliseyev, Alexei
Rukavishnikov, Nikolai
Docked with Salyut 1 but only for a short time; could not enter station

Ascent date: April 22, 1971
Descent date: April 24, 1971

SOYUZ 11 TO SALYUT 1
Crew
Dobrovolsky, Georgi
Patsayev, Viktor
Volkov, Vladislav
Crew died of asphyxiation upon reentry

Ascent date: June 6, 1971
Descent date: June 29, 1971

SOYUZ 12
Crew
Lazarev, Vasily
Makarov, Oleg

Ascent date: September 27, 1973
Descent date: September 29, 1973

SOYUZ 13 Orion 2 Space Observatory
Crew
Klimuk, Pyotr
Lebedev, Valentin

Ascent date: December 18, 1973
Descent date: December 26, 1973

SALYUT 3 SPACE STATION
Unmanned launch: June 25, 1974   Reentry: January 24, 1975

SOYUZ 14 TO SALYUT 3
Crew
Popov, Pavel
Artyukhin, Yuri

Ascent date: July 3, 1974
Descent date: July 19, 1974

SOYUZ 15 TO SALYUT 3
Crew
Sarafanov, Gennedi
Demin, Lev
Unable to dock with Salyut 3

Ascent date: August 26, 1974
Descent date: August 28, 1974

SOYUZ 16 (ASTP test)
Crew
Filipchenko, Anatoly
Rukavishnikov, Nikolai

Ascent date: December 2, 1974
Descent date: December 8, 1974

SALYUT 4 SPACE STATION
Unmanned launch: December 26, 1974   Reentry: February 3, 1977

SOYUZ 17 TO SALYUT 4
Crew
Grechko, Georgi
Guberev, Alexei

Ascent date: January 11, 1975
Descent date: February 9, 1975

SOYUZ 18a (also known as Soyuz 7K-T No.39)
Crew   date: April 5, 1975
Lazarev, Vasily
Makarov, Oleg
Suborbital only; flight of 21 minutes aborted due to a failure of the Soyuz launch vehicle.
Crew safe.

SOYUZ 18 TO SALYUT 4
Crew
Klimuk, Pyotr
Sevastyanov, Vitaly

Ascent date: May 24, 1975
Descent date: July 26, 1975

SOYUZ 19 (APOLLO-SOYUZ) Ascent date: July 16, 1975
Crew   Descent date: July 21, 1975
Leonov, Alexey
Kubasov, Valeri
Docked with US Apollo spacecraft 7/17/1975, US crew consisting of Thomas Stafford,
Vance Brand, and Donald "Deke" Slayton.

SOYUZ 20 TO SALYUT 4 Ascent date: November 17, 1975
Unmanned biological payload Descent date: February 16, 1976
Docked with Salyut 4. Long duration (3 month) test of living organisms in space.

SALYUT 5 SPACE STATION
Unmanned launch: June 22, 1976 Reentry: August 8, 1977

SOYUZ 21 TO SALYUT 5 Ascent date: July 6, 1976
Crew Descent date: August 24, 1976
Volynov, Boris
Zholobov, Vitaly

SOYUZ 22 Ascent date: September 15, 1976
Crew Descent date: September 23, 1976
Bykovsky, Valery
Aksyonov, Vladimir

SOYUZ 23 TO SALYUT 5 Ascent date: October 14, 1976
Crew Descent date: October 16, 1976
Zudov, Vyacheslav
Rozhdestvensky, Valery
Equipment malfunction; unable to dock

SOYUZ 24 TO SALYUT 5 Ascent date: February 7, 1977
Crew Descent date: February 25, 1977
Gorbatko, Viktor
Glazkov, Yuri

SALYUT 6 SPACE STATION
Unmanned launch 29 September 1977 Reentry July 29, 1982
(This Salyut had two docking ports.)

SOYUZ 25 TO SALYUT 6 Ascent date: October 9, 1977
Crew Descent date: October 11, 1977
Kovalyonok, Vladimir
Ryumin, Valery

SOYUZ 26 TO SALYUT 6 Ascent date: December 10, 1977
Ascending crew
Romanenko, Yuri
Grechko, Georgi

Descending crew   Descent date: January 16, 1978
Dzhanibekov, Vladimir
Makarov, Oleg

SOYUZ 27 TO SALYUT 6   Ascent date: January 10, 1978
Ascending crew
Dzhanibekov, Vladimir
Makarov, Oleg

Descending crew   Descent date: March 16, 1978
Romanenko, Yuri
Grechko, Georgi

SOYUZ 28 TO SALYUT 6   Ascent date: March 2, 1978
Crew   Descent date: March 10, 1978
Guberev, Alexei
Remek, Vladimir (Czechoslovakia)

SOYUZ 29 TO SALYUT 6   Ascent date: June 15, 1978
Ascending crew
Kovalyonok, Vladimir
Ivanchenkov, Aleksandr
Descending crew   Descent date: September 3, 1978
Bykovsky, Valery
Jähn, Sigmund (DDR)

SOYUZ 30 TO SALYUT 6   Ascent date: June 27, 1978
Crew   Descent date: July 5, 1978
Klimuk, Pyotr
Hermaszewski, Miroslaw (Poland)

SOYUZ 31 TO SALYUT 6   Ascent date: August 26, 1978
Ascending crew
Bykovsky, Valery
Jähn, Sigmund (DDR)
Descending crew   Descent date: November 2, 1978
Kovalyonok, Vladimir
Ivanchenkov, Aleksandr

SOYUZ 32 TO SALYUT 6   Ascent date: February 25, 1979
Crew   Descent date: June 13, 1979
Lyakhov, Vladimir
Ryumin, Valery

SOYUZ 33   TO SALYUT 6
Crew
Rukavishnikov, Nikolai
Ivanov, Georgi (Bulgaria)
Soyuz 23 was unable to dock due to engine failure

Ascent date: April 10, 1979
Descent date: April 12, 1979

SOYUZ 34   TO SALYUT 6
Unmanned ascent (with redesigned engine)

Ascent date: June 6, 1979

Descending crew
Lyakhov, Vladimir
Ryumin, Valery

Descent date: August 19, 1979

SOYUZ 35   TO SALYUT 6
Ascending crew
Popov, Leonid
Ryumin, Valery
Descending crew
Kubasov, Valeri
Farkas, Bertalan (Hungary)

Ascent date: April 9, 1980

Descent date: June 6. 1980

SOYUZ 36   TO SALYUT 6
Ascending crew
Kubasov, Valeri
Farkas, Bertalan (Hungary)
Descending crew
Gorbatko, Viktor
Tuân, Pham (Vietnam)

Ascent date: May 26, 1980

Descent date: July 31, 1980

SOYUZ T-2 TO SALYUT 6
Crew
Malyshev, Yury
Aksyonov, Vladimir

Ascent date: June 5, 1980
Descent date: June 9, 1980

SOYUZ 37 TO SALYUT 6
Ascending crew
Gorbatko, Viktor
Tuân, Pham (Vietnam)
Descending crew
Popov, Leonid
Ryumin, Valery

Ascent date: July 23, 1980
Descent date: October 11, 1980

SOYUZ 38 TO SALYUT 6
Crew
Romanenko, Yuri
Tamayo-Mendez, Arnaldo (Cuba)

Ascent date: September 18, 1980
Descent date: September 26, 1980

SOYUZ T-3 TO SALYUT 6
Crew
Kizim, Leonid
Makarov, Oleg
Strekalov, Gennady

Ascent date: November 27, 1980
Descent date: November 27, 1980

SOYUZ T-4 TO SALYUT 6
Crew
Kovalyonok, Vladimir
Savinykh, Viktor

Ascent date: March 12, 1981
Descent date: May 26, 1981

SOYUZ 39 TO SALYUT 6
Crew
Dzhanibekov, Vladimir
Gürragchaa, Jügderdemidiin (Mongolia)

Ascent date: March 22, 1981
Descent date: March 30, 1981

SOYUZ 40 TO SALYUT 6
Crew
Popov, Leonid
Prunariu, Dumitru (Romania)

Ascent date: May 14, 1981
Descent date: May 22, 1981

SALYUT 7 SPACE STATION
Unmanned launch April 19, 1982   Reentry February 7, 1991

SOYUZ T-5 TO SALYUT 7
Ascending crew
Berezovoy, Anatoli
Lebedev, Valentin
Descending crew
Popov, Leonid
Serebrov, Aleksandr
Savitskaya, Svetlana

Ascent date: May 13, 1982

Descent date: August 27, 1982

SOYUZ T-6 TO SALYUT 7
Crew
Dzhanibekov, Vladimir
Ivanchenkov, Aleksandr
Chrétien, Jean-Loup (France)

Ascent date: June 24, 1982
Descent date: July 2, 1982

SOYUZ T-7 TO SALYUT 7
Ascending crew
Popov, Leonid
Serebrov, Aleksandr
Savitskaya, Svetlana
Descending crew
Berezovoy, Anatoli
Lebedev, Valentin

Ascent date: August 19, 1982
Descent date: December 10, 1982

SOYUZ T-8 TO SALYUT 7
Crew
Titov, Vladimir
Strekalov, Gennady
Serebrov, Aleksandr
Docking was aborted due to mechanical problems.

Ascent date: April 20, 1983
Descent date: April 22, 1983

SOYUZ T-9 TO SALYUT 7
Crew
Lyakhov, Vladimir
Aleksandrov, Aleksandr

Ascent date: June 27, 1983
Descent date: November 23, 1983

SOYUZ T-10a also known as Soyuz 7K-ST No. 16L or SOYUZ T-10-1
Crew
Titov, Vladimir
Strekalov, Gennady
Not launched; rocket exploded on pad; crew escaped safely.

Launch date: September 26, 1983

SOYUZ T-10 TO SALYUT 7
Ascending crew
Kizim, Leonid
Solovyev, Vladimir
Atkov, Oleg
Descending crew
Malyshev, Yury
Strekalov, Gennady
Sharma, Rakesh (India)

Ascent date: February 8, 1984

Descent date: April 11, 1984

SOYUZ T-11 TO SALYUT 7
Ascending crew
Malyshev, Yury
Strekalov, Gennady
Sharma, Rakesh (India)

Ascent date: April 3, 1984

Descending crew
Kizim, Leonid
Solovyev, Vladimir
Atkov, Oleg

Descent date: October 3, 1984

SOYUZ T-12 TO SALYUT 7
Crew
Dzhanibekov, Vladimir
Savitskaya, Svetlana
Volk, Igor

Ascent date: July 17, 1984
Descent date: July 29, 1984

SOYUZ T-13 TO SALYUT 7
Ascending crew
Dzhanibekov, Vladimir
Savinykh, Viktor
Descending crew
Dzhanibekov, Vladimir
Grechko, Georgi

Ascent date: June 6, 1985

Descent date: September 26, 1985

SOYUZ T-14 TO SALYUT 7
Ascending crew
Vasyutin, Vladimir
Grechko, Georgi
Volkov, Alexander
Descending crew
Vasyutin, Vladimir
Volkov, Alexander
Savinykh, Viktor

Ascent date: September 17, 1985

Descent date: November 21, 1985

MIR SPACE STATION
1986-2001

Unmanned Mir launch in modules began on February 20, 1986 through April 23, 1996. It was administered by the new Russian Federal Space Agency (RKA) after the collapse of the USSR. Mir was abandoned and fell back to earth in March 2001 after funding was cut off.

SOYUZ T-15 TO SALYUT 7   AND MIR
Crew
Kizim, Leonid
Solovyev, Vladimir

Ascent date: March 13, 1986
Descent date: July 16, 1986

SOYUZ TM-1 TO MIR Ascent date: May 21, 1986
Unmanned test flight of new Soyuz-TM spacecraft. Descent date: May 30, 1986

SOYUZ TM-2 TO MIR Ascent date: February 5, 1987
Ascending crew
Romanenko, Yuri
Laveykin, Aleksandr
Descending crew Descent date: July 30, 1987
Laveykin, Aleksandr
Viktorenko, Aleksandr
Faris, Muhammed (Syria)

SOYUZ TM-3 TO MIR Ascent date: July 22, 1987
Ascending crew
Viktorenko, Aleksandr
Aleksandrov, Aleksandr Pavlovich
Faris, Muhammed (Syria)
Descending crew Descent date:: December 29, 1987
Romanenko, Yuri
Aleksandrov, Aleksandr Pavlovich
Levchenko, Anatoli

SOYUZ TM-4 TO MIR Ascent date: December 21, 1987
Ascending crew
Titov, Vladimir
Manarov, Musa
Levchenko, Anatoli
Descending crew Descent date: June 17, 1988
Solovyev, Anatoly
Savinykh, Viktor
Aleksandrov, Aleksandr (Bulgaria)

SOYUZ TM-5 TO MIR Ascent date: June 7, 1988
Ascending crew
Solovyev, Anatoly
Savinykh, Viktor
Aleksandrov, Aleksandr (Bulgaria)
Descending crew Descent date: September 7, 1988
Lyakhov, Vladimir
Mohmand, Abdul Ahad (Afghanistan)

SOYUZ TM-6 TO MIR   Ascent date: August 29, 1988
Crew
Lyakhov, Vladimir
Polyakov, Valeri
Mohmand, Abdul Ahad (Afghanistan)
Descending crew   Descent date: December 21, 1988
Titov, Vladimir
Manarov, Musa
Chrétien, Jean-Loup (France)

SOYUZ TM-7 TO MIR   Ascent date: November 26, 1988
Ascending crew
Volkov, Alexander
Krikalev, Sergei
Chrétien, Jean-Loup (France)
Descending crew   Descent date: April 27, 1989
Volkov, Alexander
Krikalev, Sergei
Polyakov, Valeri

SOYUZ TM-8 TO MIR   Ascent date: September 5, 1989
Crew   Descent date: February 19, 1990
Viktorenko, Aleksandr
Serebrov, Aleksandr

SOYUZ TM-9 TO MIR   Ascent date: February 11, 1990
Crew   Descent date: August 9, 1990
Solovyev, Anatoly
Balandin, Aleksandr

SOYUZ TM-10 TO MIR   Ascent date: August 1, 1990
Ascending crew
Manakov, Gennadi
Strekalov, Gennadi
Descending crew   Descent date: December 10, 1990
Manakov, Gennadi
Strekalov, Gennadi
Akiyama, Toyohiro (Japan)

SOYUZ TM-11 TO MIR   Ascent date: December 2, 1990
Ascending crew
Afanasyev, Viktor
Manarov, Musa
Akiyama, Toyohiro (Japan)
Descending crew   Descent date: May 26, 1991
Afanasyev, Viktor
Manarov, Musa
Sharman, Helen (UK)

SOYUZ TM-12 TO MIR   Ascent date: May 18, 1991
Ascending crew
Artsebarsky, Anatoly
Krikalev, Sergei
Sharman, Helen (UK)
Descending crew   Descent date: October 10, 1991
Artsebarsky, Anatoly
Aubakirov, Toktar (Kazakhstan)
Viehböck, Franz (Austria)

SOYUZ TM-13 TO MIR   Ascent date: October 2, 1991
Ascending crew
Volkov, Alexander
Aubakirov, Toktar (Kazakhstan)
Viehböck, Franz (Austria)
Descending crew   Descent date: March 25, 1992
Volkov, Alexander
Krikalev, Sergei
Flade, Klaus-Dietrich (Germany)

SOYUZ TM-14 TO MIR   Ascent date: March 17, 1992
Ascending crew
Viktorenko, Aleksandr
Kaleri, Alexander
Flade, Klaus-Dietrich (Germany)
Descending crew   Descent date: August 10, 1992
Viktorenko, Aleksandr
Kaleri, Alexander
Tognini, Michel (France)

SOYUZ TM-15 TO MIR
Crew
Solovyev, Anatoly
Avdeyev, Sergei
Tognini, Michel (France)

Ascent date: July 27, 1992
Descent date: February 1, 1993

SOYUZ TM-16 TO MIR
Ascending crew
Manakov, Gennadi
Poleshchuk, Alexander
Descending crew
Manakov, Gennadi
Poleshchuk, Alexander
Haigneré, Jean-Pierre (France)

Ascent date: January 24, 1993

Descent date: July 22, 1993

SOYUZ TM-17 TO MIR
Ascending crew
Tsibliyev, Vasili
Serebrov, Aleksandr
Haigneré, Jean-Pierre (France)
Descending crew
Tsibliyev, Vasili
Serebrov, Aleksandr

Ascent date: July 1, 1993

Descent date: January 14, 1994

SOYUZ TM-18 TO MIR
Ascending crew
Afanasyev, Viktor
Usachov, Yury
Polyakov, Valeri
Descending crew
Afanasyev, Viktor
Usachov, Yury

Ascent date: January 8, 1994

Descent date: July 9, 1994

Beginning in 1994, some US Space Shuttle missions began launches to Mir and the ISS, but listed here are only those that include Russian crew members.

STS-60 SHUTTLE TO ISS
Crew
Bolden, Charles
Reightler, Kenneth
Davis, Jan
Sega, Ron
Chang-Diaz, Franklin
Krikalev, Sergei

Ascent date: February 3, 1994
Descent date: December 13, 1994
Carried SPACEHAB module to ISS

SOYUZ TM-19 TO MIR
Ascending crew   Ascent date: July 1, 1994
Malechenko, Yuri
Musabayev, Talgat
Descending crew   Descent date: November 4, 1994
Malechenko, Yuri
Musabayev, Talgat
Merbold, Ulf (Germany)

SOYUZ TM-20 TO MIR
Ascending crew   Ascent date: October 3, 1994
Viktorenko, Alexander
Kondakove, Yelena
Merbold, Ulf (Germany)
Descending crew   Descent date: March 22, 1995
Viktorenko, Alexander
Kondakova, Yelena
Polyakov, Valery

STS-63 SHUTTLE TO ISS AND MIR   Ascent date: February 3, 1995
Crew   Descent date: February 12, 1995
Wetherbee, James
Collins, Eileen
Foale, Michael   (Performed fly-around of Mir.)
Voss, Janice
Harris, Bernard
Titov, Vladimir

SOYUZ TM-21 TO MIR
Ascending Crew   Ascent date: March 14, 1995
Dezhurov, Vladimir
Strekalov, Gennadi
Thagard, Norm (USA)
Descending crew   Descent date: September 11, 1995
Solovyov, Anatoly   (Descent crew was from Shuttle STS-71)
Budarin, Nikolai

STS-71 SHUTTLE TO MIR   Ascent date: September 7, 1995
Crew
Gibson, Robert
Precourt, Charles
Baker, Ellen
Dunbar, Bonnie

Harbaugh, Gregory
Dezhurov, Vladimir
Solovyov, Anatoly
Budarin, Nikolai
Descending crew   Descent date: September 18, 1995
Gibson, Robert
Precourt, Charles
Baker, Ellen
Dunbar, Bonnie
Harbaugh, Gregory
Thagard, Norman (USA)
Dezhurov, Vladimir
Strekalov, Gennadi

SOYUZ TM-22 TO MIR
Ascending crew   Ascent date: September 3, 1995
Gidzenko, Yuri
Avdeyev, Sergei
Reiter, Thomas (Germany)

Descending crew   Descent date: February 29, 1996
Gidzenko, Yuri
Avdeyev, Sergei
Reiter, Thomas (Germany)

SOYUZ TM-23 TO MIR
Ascending crew   Ascent date: February 21, 1996
Onofrienko, A
Usachov, Yuri
Descending crew   Descent date: September 2, 1996
Onofrienko, A
Usachov, Yuri
Andre-Deshays, Claudie (France)

SOYUZ TM-24 TO MIR
Ascending crew   Ascent date: August 17, 1996
Korzun, Valery
Kaleri, Alexander
Andre-Deshays, Claudie (France)
Descending crew   Descent date: March 2, 1997
Korzun, Valery
Kaleri, Alexander
Ewald, Reinhold (Germany)

SOYUZ TM-25 TO MIR
Ascending crew   Ascent date: February 10, 1997
Tsibliyev, Vasily
Lazutkin, Aleksandr
Ewald, Reinhold (Germany)
Descending crew   Descent date: August 14, 1997
Tsibliyev, Vasily
Lazutkin, Aleksandr

STS-84 SHUTTLE TO MIR   Ascent date: May 15, 1997
Crew   Descent: May 25, 1997
Precourt, Charles
Collins, Eileen
Noriega, Carlos
Lu, Edward
Clervoy, Jean-François
Kondakova, Yelena
Foale, Michael (remained on Mir)
Linenger, Jerry (returned from Mir from STS-81)

SOYUZ TM-26 TO MIR
Ascending crew   Ascent date: August 5, 1997
Solovyov, Anatoly
Vinogradov, Pavel
Descending crew   Descent date: February 19, 1998
Solovyov, Anatoly
Vinogradov, Pavel
Eyharts, Leopold (France)

STS-87 SHUTTLE   Ascent date: November 19, 1997
Crew   Descent date: December 5, 1997
Kregel, Kevin
Lindsey, Steven
Scott, Winston
Chawla, Kalpana
Doi, Takao (Japan)
Kadenyuk. Leonid (Ukraine)

STS-89 SHUTTLE TO MIR   Ascent date: January 22, 1998
Crew   Descent date: January 31, 1998
Wilcutt, Terence
Edwards, John
Dunbar, Bonnie

Anderson, Michael
Reilly, James
Sharipov, Salizhan (Russia)
Thomas, Andrew (remained on Mir)
Wolf, David (returned from Mir)

SOYUZ TM-27 TO MIR

Ascending crew   Ascent date: January 29, 1998
Musabayev, Talgat
Budarin, Nikolai
Eyharts, Leopold (France)
Descending crew   Descent date: August 25, 1998
Musabayev, Talgat
Budarin, Nikolai
Baturin, Yuri

STS-96 SHUTTLE TO ISS

Crew   Ascent date: May 27, 1999
                                        Descent date: June 6, 1999
Rominger, Kent
Husband, Rick
Ochoa, Ellen
Jernigan, Tamara
Barry, Daniel
Payette, Julie
Tokarev, Valeri (Russia)

SOYUZ TM-28 TO MIR

Ascending crew   Ascent date: August 13, 1998
Padalka, Gennady
Avdeyev, Sergei
Baturin, Yuri
Descending crew   Descent date: February 28, 1999
Padalka, Gennady
Bella, Ivan (Czechoslovakia)

SOYUZ TM-29 TO MIR

Ascending crew   Ascent date: February 20, 1999
Afansayev, Viktor
Haignere, Jean-Pierre (France)
Bella, Ivan (Czechoslovakia)
Descending crew   Descent date: August 28, 1999
Afansayev, Viktor
Avdeyev, Sergei
Haignere, Jean-Pierre (France)

SOYUZ TM-30 TO MIR

Crew
Zalyotin, Sergei
Kaleri, Alexander

Ascent date: April 4, 2000
(Final visit to Mir)
Descent date: June 16, 2000

THE REMAINING LISTING OF SPACE MISSIONS ARE ALL TO THE INTERNATIONAL SPACE STATION UNLESS NOTED OTHERWISE.

STS-101 SHUTTLE

Crew
Halsell, James
Horowitz, Scott
Weber, Mary
Williams, Jeffrey
Voss, Jams
Helms, Susan
Usachev, Yury (Russia)

Ascent date: May 19, 2000
Descent date: May 29, 2000

STS-106 SHUTTLE

Crew
Wilcutt, Terrence
Altman, Scott
Burbank, Daniel
Lu, Edward
Mastracchio, Richard
Malenchenko, Yuri (Russia)
Morukov, Boris (Russia)

Ascent date: September 8, 2000
Descent date: September 20, 2000

SOYUZ TM-31

Ascending crew
Gidzenko, Yuri
Krikalev, Sergei
Shepherd, William (USA)
Descending crew
Musabayev, Talgat
Baturin, Yuri
Tito, Dennis (USA, 1st Space Tourist)

Ascent date: October 31, 2000
(1st crew to man ISS)

Descent date: May 6, 2001

STS-102 SHUTTLE

Ascending Crew
Wetherbee, James
Kelly, James
Thomas, Andrew

Ascent date: March 8, 2001

Richards, Paul
Voss, James
Helms, Susan
Usachev, Yuru (Russia)
Descending crew   Descent date: March 21, 2001
Wetherbee, James
Kelly, James
Thomas, Andrew
Richards, Paul
Shepherd, William
Gidzenko, Yuri (Russia)
Krikalev, Sergei (Russia)

STS-100 SHUTTLE   Ascent date: April 19, 2001
Crew   Descent date: May 1, 2001
Rominger, Kent
Ashby, Jeffrey
Hadfield, Chris (Canada)
Parazynski, Scott
Phillips, John
Guidoni, Umberto (Italy)
Lonchakov, Yuri

SOYUZ TM-32
Ascending crew   Ascent date: April 25, 2001
Musabayev, Talgat
Baturin, Yuri
Tito, Dennis (USA, 1st Space Tourist)
Descending crew   Descent date: October 31, 2001
Afansayev, Viktor
Haignere, Jean-Pierre (France)
Kozeyev, Konstantin

STS-105 SHUTTLE   Ascent date: August 10, 2001
Ascending crew
Horowitz, Scott
Sturckow, Frederick
Barry, Daniel
Forrester, Patrick
Culbertson, Frank
Turyin, Mikhail (Russia)
Dezhurov, Vladimir (Russia)

Descending crew   Descent date: October 21, 2001
Horowitz, Scott
Sturckow, Frederick
Barry, Daniel
Forrester, Patrick
Culbertson, Frank
Usachev, Yury (Russia)
Voss, James
Helms, Susan

SOYUZ TM-33
Ascending crew   Ascent date: October 21, 2001
Afansayev, Viktor
Haignere, Jean-Pierre (France)
Kozeyev, Konstantin
Descending crew   Descent date: May 5, 2002
Gidzenko, Yuri
Vittori, Roberto (Italy)
Shuttleworth, Mark (South Africa, 2nd Space Tourist)

STS-108 SHUTTLE
Ascending crew   Ascent date: December 5, 2001
Gorie, Dominic
Kelly, Mark
Godwin, Linda
Tani, Daniel
Onufrienko, Yuri (Russia)
Walz, Carl
Bursch, Daniel
Descending crew   Descent date: December 17, 2001
Gorie, Dominic
Kelly, Mark
Godwin, Linda
Tani, Daniel
Culbertson, Frank
Turyin, Mikhail (Russia)
Dezhurov, Vladimir (Russia)

SOYUZ TM-34
Ascending crew   Ascent date: April 25, 2002
Gidzenko, Yuri
Vittori, Roberto (Italy)
Shuttleworth, Mark (South Africa, 2nd Space Tourist)

Descending crew
Zalyotin, Sergei
Lonchakov, Yury
De Winne, Frank

Descent date: November 10, 2002

STS-111 SHUTTLE
Crew
Cockrell. Kenneth
Lockhart, Paul
Chang-Diaz, Franklin
Perrin, Phillippe (France)
Korzun, Valery (Russia)
Whitson, Peggy
Treshchev, Sergei (Russia)
Descending crew
Cockrell. Kenneth
Lockhart, Paul
Chang-Diaz, Franklin
Perrin, Phillippe (France)
Onufrienko, Yuri (Russia)
Walz, Carl
Bursch, Daniel

Ascent date: June 5, 2002

Descent date: June 19, 2002

STS-112 SHUTTLE
Crew
Ashby, Jeffrey
Melroy, Pamela
Wolf, David
Sellers, Piers
Magnus, Sandra
Yurchikhin, Fyodor (Russia)

Ascent date: October 7, 2002
Descent date: October 18, 2002

SOYUZ TMA-1
Ascending crew
Zalyotin, Sergei
Lonchakov, Yury
De Winne, Frank
Descending crew
Baturin, Yuri
Bowersox, Kenneth (USA)
Pettit, Donald (USA)

Ascent date: October 30, 2002

Descent date: May 4, 2003
Returned American crewman from STS-113

STS-113 SHUTTLE
Ascending crew
Wetherbee, James
Lockhart, Paul
Lopez-Algeria, Michael
Herrington, John
Bowersox, Kenneth
Budarin, Nikolai (Russia)
Pettit, Donald
Descending crew
Wetherbee, James
Lockhart, Paul
Lopez-Algeria, Michael
Herrington, John
Korzun, Valery (Russia)
Whitson, Peggy
Treshchev, Sergei (Russia)

Ascent date: November 23, 2002

Descent date: December 7, 2002

After STS-113, no more shuttle missions carried any Russian crewmen.

SOYUZ TMA-2
Ascending crew
Malechenko, Yuri
Lu, Edward (USA)
Descending crew
Malechenko, Yuri
Lu, Edward (USA)
Duque, Pedro (Spain)

Ascent date: April 26, 2003

Descent date: October 28, 2003

SOYUZ TMA-3
Ascending crew
Kaleri, Aleksandr
Duque, Pedro (Spain)
Foale, Michael (USA)
Descending crew
Kaleri, Aleksandr
Foale, Michael (USA)
Kuipers, André (Netherlands)

Ascent date: October 8, 2003

Descent date: April 30, 2004

SOYUZ TMA-4
Ascending crew
Padalka, Gennady
Fincke, Michael (USA)
Kuipers, André (Netherlands)

Ascent date: April 18, 2004

Descending crew   Descent date: October 24, 2004
Padalka, Gennady
Fincke, Michael (USA)
Shargin, Yuri

SOYUZ TMA-5
Ascending crew   Ascent date: October 14, 2004
Sharipov, Salizhan
Chaio, Leroy (USA)
Shargin, Yuri
Descending crew   Descent date: April 24, 2005
Sharipov, Salizhan
Chaio, Leroy (USA**)**
Vittori, Roberto (Italy)

SOYUZ TMA-6
Ascending crew   Ascent date: April 15, 2005
Krikalev, Sergei
Phillips, John USA
Vittori, Roberto (Italy)
Descending crew   Descent date: October 11, 2005
Krikalev, Sergei
Phillips, John (USA)
Olsen, Gregory (USA, 3rd Space Tourist)

SOYUZ TMA-7
Ascending crew   Ascent date: October 1, 2005
Tokarev, Valeri
Mc Arthur, William (USA)
Olsen, Gregory (USA, 3rd Space Tourist)
Descending crew   Descent date: April 8, 2006
Tokarev, Valeri
Mc Arthur, William (USA)
Pontes, Marcos (Brazil)

SOYUZ TMA-8
Ascending crew   Ascent date: March 30, 2006
Vinogradov, Pavel
Williams, Jeffrey
Pontes, Marcos (Brazil)
Descending crew   Descent date: September 29, 2006
Vinogradov, Pavel
Williams, Jeffrey (USA)
Ansari, Anousheh (Iranian American, 4th Space Tourist)

SOYUZ TMA-9

Ascending crew   Ascent date: September 18, 2006
Tyurin, Mikhail
Lopez-Algeria, Michael (USA)
Ansari, Anousheh (Iranian American, 4th Space Tourist)
Descending crew   Descent date:April 21, 2007
Tyurin, Mikhail
Lopez-Algeria, Michael (USA)
Simonyi, Charles (USA Hungarian-born, 5th Space Tourist)

SOYUZ TMA-10

Ascending crew   Ascent date: April 7, 2007
Kotov, Oleg (Ukraine)
Yurchikchin, Fyodor
Simonyi, Charles (USA Hungarian-born, 5th Space Tourist)
Descending crew   Descent date: October 21, 2007
Kotov, Oleg (Ukraine)
Yurchikchin, Fyodor
Shukor, Sheikh Muszaphar (Malaysia)

SOYUZ TMA-11

Ascending crew   Ascent date: October 10, 2007
Melenchenko, Yuri
Whitson, Peggy (USA)
Shukor, Sheikh Muszaphar (Malaysia)
Descending crew   Descent date: April 19, 2008
Melenchenko, Yuri
Whitson, Peggy (USA)
Yi, So-yeon (South Korea)

SOYUZ TMA-12

Ascending crew   Ascent date: April 8, 2008
Volkov, Sergey
Kononenko, Oleg
Yi, So-yeon (South Korea)
Descending crew   Descent date: October 24, 2008
Volkov, Sergey
Kononenko, Oleg
Garriott, Richard (USA, 6th Space Tourist)

SOYUZ TMA-13

Ascending crew   Ascent date: October 12, 2008
Lonchakov, Yury
Fincke, Michael (USA)
Garriott, Richard (USA, 6th Space Tourist)

Descending crew   Descent date: April 8, 2009
Lonchakov, Yury
Fincke, Michael (USA)
Simonyi, Charles (USA Hungarian-born, 7th Space Tourist, second trip)

SOYUZ TMA-14
Ascending crew   Ascent date: March 26, 2009
Padalka, Gennady
Barrett, Michael (USA)
Simonyi, Charles (USA Hungarian-born, 7th Space Tourist, second trip)
Descending crew   Descent date: October 11, 2009
Padalka, Gennady
Barrett, Michael (USA)
Laliberté, Guy (Canada, 8th Space Tourist)

SOYUZ TMA-15
Crew   Ascent date: May 27, 2009
Romanenko, Roman   Descent date: December 1, 2009
De Winne, Frank (Belgium)
Thirsk, Robert (Canada)

SOYUZ TMA-16
Ascending crew   Ascent date: September 30, 2009
Suryev, Maksim
Williams, Jeffrey (USA)
Laliberté, Guy (Canada, 8th Space Tourist)
Descending crew   Descent date: March 18, 2010
Suryev, Maksim
Williams, Jeffrey (USA)

SOYUZ TMA-17
Crew   Ascent date: December 20, 2009
Kotov, Oleg (Ukrainian)   Descent date: June 2, 2010
Creamer, Thomas (USA)
Noguchi, Soichi (Japan)

SOYUZ TMA-18
Crew   Ascent date: April 2, 2010
Skvortsov Aleksandr   Descent date: September 25, 2010
Korniyenko, Mikhail
Caldwell, Tracy (USA)

SOYUZ TMA-19

Crew
Yurchikchin, Fyodor
Walker, Shannon (USA)
Wheelock, Douglas (USA)

Ascent date: June 15, 2010
Descent date: November 26, 2010

SOYUZ TMA-01M

Crew
Kaleri, Aleksandr
Skripochka, Oleg
Kelly, Scott (USA)

Ascent date: October 7, 2010
Descent date: March 16, 2011

SOYUZ TMA-20

Crew
Kondratyev, Dmitri
Coleman, Catherine "Cady" (USA)
Nespoli, Paolo (Italy)

Ascent date: December 15, 2010
Descent date: May 24, 2011

SOYUZ TMA-21

Crew
Samokutyayev, Aleksandr
Borisenko, Andrei
Garan, Ronald (USA)

Ascent date: April 4, 2011
Descent date: September 16, 2011

SOYUZ TMA-02M

Crew
Volkov, Sergey
Fossum, Michael (USA)
Furukawa, Satoshi (Japan)

Ascent date: June 7, 2011
Descent date: November 22, 2011

SOYUZ TMA-22

Crew
Shkaplerov, Anton
Ivanishin, Anatoli
Burbank, Daniel (USA)

Ascent date: November 14, 2011
Descent date: April 27, 2012

SOYUZ TMA-03M

Ascending crew
Kononenko, Oleg
Kuipers, André (Netherlands)
Pettit, Donald (USA)

Ascent date: December 21, 2011
Descent date: July 1, 2012

SOYUZ TMA-04M

Padalka, Gennady
Revin, Sergei
Acaba, Joseph (USA)

Ascent date: May 15, 2012
Descent date: September 17, 2012

SOYUZ TMA-05M

Crew
Malenchenko, Yuri
Williams, Sunita (USA)
Hoshide, Akihiko (Japan)

Ascent date: July 15 2012
Descent date: November 19, 2012

SOYUZ TMA-06M

Crew
Novitski, Oleg
Tarelkin, Evgeny
Ford, Kevin (USA)

Ascent date: October 23, 2012
Descent date: March 16, 2013

SOYUZ TMA-07M

Crew
Romanenko, Roman
Marshburn, Thomas (USA)
Hadfield, Chris (Canada)

Ascent date: December 12, 2012
Descent date: May 14, 2013

SOYUZ TMA-08M

Crew
Vinogradov, Pavel
Misurkin, Alexander
Cassidy, Christopher

Ascent date: March 28, 2013
Descent date: September 11, 2013

SOYUZ TMA-09M

Crew
Yurchikchin, Fyodor
Nyberg, Karen (USA)
Parmitano, Luca (Italy)

Ascent date: May 28, 2013
Descent date: November 11, 2013

SOYUZ TMA-10M

Crew
Kotov, Oleg (Ukrainian)
Ryazanski, Sergey
Hopkins, Michael (USA)

Ascent date: September 25, 2013
Descent date: March 11, 2014

SOYUZ TMA-11M

Crew
Tyurin, Mikhail
Mastracchio, Richard (USA)
Wakata, Koichi (Japan)

Ascent date: November 7, 2013
Descent date: May 14, 2014

SOYUZ TMA-12M

Crew
Skvortsov, Aleksandr
Artemyev, Oleg
Swanson, Steven

Ascent date: March 25, 2014
Descent date: September 11, 2014

SOYUZ TMA-13M

Crew
Suryev, Maksim
Wiseman, Gregory (USA)
Gerst, Alexander (Germany)

Ascent date: May 28, 2014
Descent date: November 10, 2014

SOYUZ TMA-14M

Crew
Samokutyayev, Aleksandr
Serova, Yelena
Wilmore, Barry (USA)

Ascent date: September 25, 2014
Descent date: March 12, 2015

SOYUZ TMA-15M

Crew
Shkaplerov, Anton
Christoforetti, Samantha (Italy)
Virts, Terry (USA)

Ascent date: November 23, 2014
Descent date: June 11, 2015

SOYUZ TMA-16M

Ascending crew
Padalka, Gennady
Korniyenko, Mikhail
Kelly, Scott (USA)
Descending crew
Padalka, Gennady
Morgensen, Andreas (Denmark)
Aimbetov, Aidyn (Kazakstan)

Ascent date: March 27, 2015

Descent date: September 12, 2015

SOYUZ TMA-17M

Crew
Kononenko, Oleg
Yui, Kimiya (Japan)
Lindgren, Kjell (USA)

Ascent date: July 22, 2015
Descent date: December 11, 2015

SOYUZ TMA-18M

Ascending crew	Ascent date: September 2, 2015
Volkov, Sergey	
Morgensen, Andreas (Denmark)	
Aimbetov, Aidyn (Kazakstan)	
Descending crew	Descent date: March 2, 2016
Volkov, Sergey	
Korniyenko, Mikhail	
Kelly, Scott (USA)	

SOYUZ TMA-19M

Crew	Ascent date: December 15, 2015
Malenchenko, Yuri	Descent date: June 18, 2016
Korpa, Timothy (USA)	
Peake, Timothy (Great Britain)	

SOYUZ TMA-20M

Crew	Ascent date: March 18, 2016
Ovchinin, Aleksey	Descent date: September 7, 2016
Skripochka, Oleg	
Williams, Jeffrey (USA)	

SOYUZ MS-01

Crew	Ascent date: July 7, 2016
Ivanishin, Anatoli	Descent date: October 30, 2016
Onishi, Takuya (Japan)	
Rubins, Kathleen (USA)	

SOYUZ MS-02

Crew	Ascent date: October 19,2016
Ryzhikov, Sergey	Descent date: April 10, 2017
Borisenko, Andrei	
Kimbrough, Robert (USA)	

SOYUZ MS-03

Crew	Ascent date: November 17, 2016
Novitskiy, Oleg	Descent date: June 2, 2017
Pesquet, Thomas (France)	
Whitson, Peggy (USA) (Ascent only)	

SOYUZ MS-04

Ascending crew (2 only)	Ascent date: April 20, 2017
Yurchikchin, Fyodor	
Fischer, Jack (USA)	

Descending crew
Yurchikchin, Fyodor
Fischer, Jack (USA)
Whitson, Peggy (USA)

Descent date: September 3, 2017

SOYUZ MS-05
Crew
Ryazanski, Sergey
Nespoli, Paolo (Italy)
Bresnik, Randy (USA)

Ascent date: July 28, 2017
Descent date: December 14, 2017

SOYUZ MS-06
Crew
Misurkin, Alexander
Vande Hei, Mark (USA)
Acaba, Joseph (USA)

Ascent date: September 12, 2017
Descent date: February 28, 2018

SOYUZ MS-07
Crew
Shkaplerov, Anton
Kanai, Norishiga (Japan)
Tingle, Scott (USA)

Ascent date: December 17, 2017
Descent date: June 3, 2018

SOYUZ MS-08
Crew
Artemyev, Oleg
Feustel, Andrew (USA)
Arnold, Richard (USA)

Ascent date: March 21, 2018
Currently in space

SOYUZ MS-09
Crew   Ascent date: June 6, 2018
Prokopyev, Sergey   Currently in space
Auñón-Chancellor, Serena (USA)
Gerst, Alexander (USA)

SOYUZ MS-10*
Scheduled crew
Ovchinin, Aleksey
Tikhornov, Nikolai
Hague, Nick (USA)

SOYUZ MS-11*
Scheduled crew
Konenenko, Oleg
Saint-Jacques, David (Canada)
McClain, Anne (USA)

SOYUZ MS-12*
Scheduled crew:
Skripchka, Oleg
Babkin, Andrei
Walker, Shannon (USA)

SOYUZ MS-13*
Scheduled crew:
Skvortsov, Aleksandr

Parmitano, Luca (Italy)
Morgan, Andrew (USA)

*Subject to change.

If you wish to write to a cosmonaut and request an autograph, address your request to:

(Name of Cosmonaut)
Lyotchik Cosmonavt
Yuri Gagarin Cosmonaut Training Centre
141 130 Zvezdny Gorodok
Moskovski Oblast
Potcha Lyotchikov Kosmonavtot
Russia – C I S

All Russian cosmonauts still living can be reached through this address. Your requests will be forwarded to those who have retired and are no longer active. Note that your request may take time for a response (as much as 3 years have been recorded by several collectors). It would be appropriate to send mint Russian stamps, or a small amount of currency to cover return postage, especially for the retired cosmonauts.

THE RUSSIAN CYRILLIC ALPHABET WITH PRONUNCIATION

А а (A)	Р р (R)
Б б (B)	С с (S)
В в (V)	Т т (T)
Г г (G)	У у (U)
Д д (D)	Ф ф (F)
Е е (E)	Х х (KH)
Ё ё (YO)	Ц ц (TS)
Ж ж (ZH)	Ч ч (CH)
З з (Z)	Ш ш (SH)
И и (I)	Щ щ (SHCH)
Й й (Y)	ъ (–)
К к (K)	ы (Y)
Л л (L)	ь (')
М м (M)	Э э (E)
Н н (N)	Ю ю (YU or IU)
О о (O)	Я я (YA or IA)
П п (P)	

PART IV

People's Republic of China
Manned Spaceflight Program

This section is designed to aid in identification of the missions and autographs of the Chinese Taikonauts. The People's Republic of China is relatively new to space exploration, having sent up its first recoverable satellite in 1975, eighteen years after the Soviet Union launched the first orbital satellite, Sputnik 1. They began their manned spaceflight program in 2003 and have since launched six manned spacecraft. As they continue with their manned spacecraft program, it is important to document their progress as much as possible. There have been many collectible space items issued since 1975, mostly in Chinese only, although some collectible covers have English translations printed on the reverse.

I am listing missions, crews, and signed covers together to assist collectors not familiar with the Chinese alphabet to better identify and verify authenticity of signed items they might obtain on the open market, such as covers or photographs of these space travelers. I'm using an entirely different format here than I used for the first part of this book to better illustrate these autographs. The Chinese government controls issuance of signed covers and it is an offense punishable by death for a Chinese citizen to forge an autograph.

Shenzhou Spacecraft Program

The first four unmanned test flights of the ShenZhou series spacecraft took place in 1999, 2001 and 2002. They are not listed here. The first manned launch followed on 12 October 2005. It was launched on the Long March 2F from the Jiuquan Satellite Launch Center. The command center controlling all missions is the Beijing Aerospace Command and Control Center. The China Manned Space Engineering Office provides engineering and administrative support for the manned Shenzhou missions. There are 14 domestic tracking stations throughout China, and they utilize 4 overseas tracking sites, and have 4 other shared facilities.

Shenzhou-5

Shenzhou-5 was launched on October 15, 2003, which carried their first astronaut, **Yang Liwei** into orbit. Landing date; 15 October 2003. The spacecraft orbited the Earth 14 times. With this launch, China became the third country in the world to have the capabilities for independent human spaceflight.

Yang Liwei signed cover

Shenzhou-6, with a crew of 2, **Fèi Jùnlóng** and **Niè Haishèng**, was launched on October 12, 2005. Landing date: October 16, 2005.

Cover signed by Fèi Jùnlóng (left) and Niè Haishèng (right)

Shenzhou-7 was launched on 25 September 2008 with a crew of 3, **Zhai Zhigang**, **Liu Boming** and **Jing Haipeng.**. Landing date: 28 September 2008. **Zhai Zhigang** performed China's first space walk.

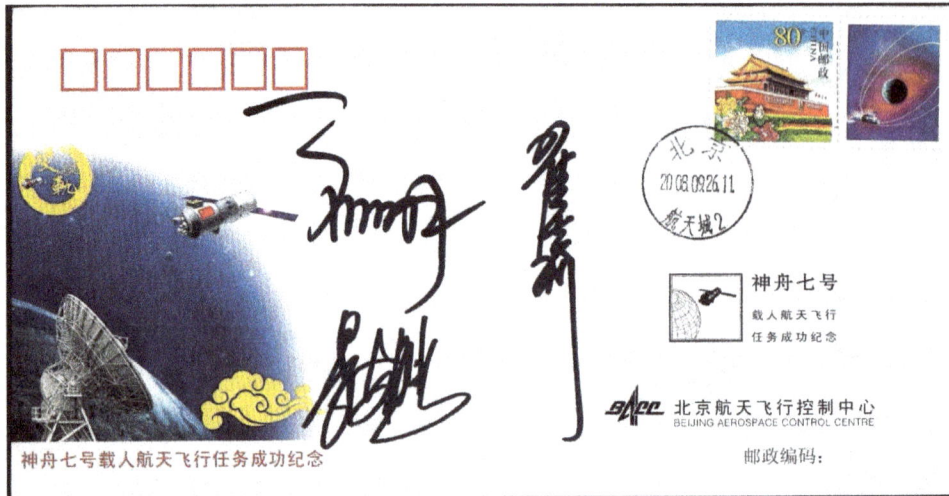

Cover signed by Liu Boming (UL), Jing Haipeng (LL) and Zhai Zhigang (R)

Tiangong-1, China's first prototype space station, was placed into orbit on 29 September 2011 Reentry: 4 April 2018 **Shenzhou-8** (unmanned) was launched on 31 October 2011. Docking with **Tiangong-1** on 2 November 2011, and undocking date: 14 November 2011. Landing date: 17 November 2011.

Shenzhou-9 craft was launched on 16 June 2012 with a crew of 3, **Jing Haipeng, Liu Wang** and **Liu Yang**, docked with the first space lab, **Tiangong-1** on 18 June 2012. This was **Jing Haipeng's** second trip into space. **Liu Yang** is the first Chinese women space traveler.

Cover signed by Liu Yang (L), Jing Haipeng (C) and Liu Wang (R)

Shenzhou-10, launched on 11 June 2013, with a crew of 3, **Nie Haisheng**, **Zhang Xiaoguang** and **Wang Yaping**. Docking date: 13 June 2013. Landing date: 26 June 2013.

Cover signed by Nie Haisheng (L), Zhang Xiaoguang (C) and Wang Yaping

A second space lab, **Tiangong-2**, was launched on 15 September 2016 to replace **Tiangong-1**.

Shenzhou-11 launched on 16 October 2016 with a crew of 2, **Jing Haipeng** and **Chen Dong** and docked with **Tiangong-2** on October 18, 2016, Landing date: 18 November 2016.

Cover signed by Jing Haipeng and Chen Dong

Shenzhou-12 is currently scheduled for launch in 2019, and China National Space Administration is planning manned expeditions to the Moon, and an unmanned mission to Mars.

Covers shown here are from an ebay seller, Shi Ning, doing business as "China Aerospace", who has available similar covers as shown above, plus a large inventory of other unsigned covers, signed photos, etc. Illustrations here have been used with permission. Tracking station covers, flown covers and tracking ship covers are also available.

Recommendations for further study and research

THE SPACE UNIT
www.space-unit.com

I highly recommend this group. The Space Unit is an organization of hobbyists devoted to the collection and study of covers and stamps issued on space themes. They have a worldwide membership and it is the largest independent astrophilatelic society in the world. They have periodic auctions of member items, and publish "The Astrophile", an outstanding periodical with many informative articles about the hobby.

CollectSpace is a news publication and online community for space enthusiasts and professionals. The site's readership includes curators and conservatores, authors and space memorabilia collectors. Visit their website at www.collectspace.com. Great information is available along with expert advise on many issues and questions.

BOB McLEOD'S ASTRONAUT AUTOGRAPH GALLERY

Visit Bob's website at www.picturetrail.com/astronautgallery and you will find: (1) Autographs of all 385 astronauts who have flown on US/NASA spacecraft (2) Complete crew signed covers/photos for all 166 US/NASA manned spaceflights (3) Autographs and photos from the Space Shuttle Enterprise ALT Program (4) Autograph examples of all flown Cosmonauts (5) Neil Armstrong autographs (6) Apollo Moonwalker autographs (7) X-15 rocket plane pilots, plus autograph examples of everyone (over 500) who has flown in space, and more...

A final note from the author

As of this writing, there are several Soyuz launches scheduled for 2018 and 2019, possibly with new space explorers whose autographs are not included in this book. Private space companies, such as Space-X and Boeing Aerospace have unmanned launches of newly designed space plane prototypes scheduled for later this year, with manned launches to follow in 2019 or later.

A very special thanks goes to Bob McLeod who has taken much of his time to double check my work, and for the many scans he has provided. Comments can be directed to me through my website www.mitchellauthor.com.

It is my hope that someone will publish a supplement, or perhaps a new book on autographs, within the next few years. You have my permission to use anything from this book.

But the question that remains in my mind; as more individuals get the opportunity to venture into space, will this hobby remain viable, or will it die? Only you, the collector, will know. I wish you good collecting, and, as Star Trek's Mr. Spock says, "Live long and prosper."

John R. Mitchell
August, 2018

www.ingramcontent.com/pod-product-compliance
Lightning Source LLC
Chambersburg PA
CBHW080254030426
42334CB00023BA/2814

9 780692 165713